Maraposa
Quilts & projects for the home

*Valori Wells is the designer of this beautiful fabric line
inspired from her garden photography.
We had a wonderful time creating the quilts and projects for this book.
Inside you will see quilts featuring the wide border stripe,
and others that feature the many companion prints.
We have kept in mind that there are three repeats on the border stripe
and have given you plenty of projects to utilize
the remainder of this wonderful focal fabric.
On the inside back cover you can view the entire collection
of Maraposa florals that Valori has designed for Free Spirit Fabrics.
If you are looking for yardage, we have the collection featured on our web site.
Enjoy your Maraposa project and happy quilting!*

Jean Wells Keenan

Table of Contents

Basic Instructions	2
Petal Play	4
Lazy Logs	6
Market Day Tote	8
Pinwheels in the Garden	10
Color Plates	11
Hidden Treasures	15
Victoria's Garden	18
Petal Play Pillow	20
Victoria's Garden Pillow	21
Pillow Sham	21
Tablecloth	22
Placemats	23
Napkins	23

General Instructions
Please read all instructions before beginning.

CUTTING

All cutting instructions are given using the rotary cutter. When using the rotary cutter, strips are cut, then these are cut into squares, triangles, and rectangles. When you are using a mat, rotary cutter, and ruler, always place your cutting board on a table and stand over it while you cut. It will be more comfortable and you will be able to exert consistent pressure on the rotary cutter.

CUTTING STRIPS

Suppose you need a 4 1/2"x 42" strip: Align the 4 1/2" mark on the ruler at the left edge of the fabric, with the top edge of the ruler on the selvages. Make a cut by placing the rotary cutter at the bottom of the fabric and moving up to the top edge. Hold the cutter firmly and press with a consistently firm but not hard motion.

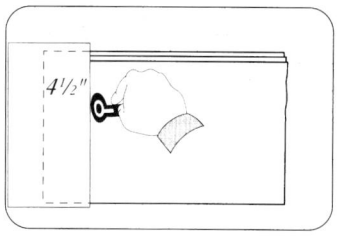

CUTTING SQUARES

Open up the strip of fabric that you just cut. You may stack four rows of strips if you wish. Trim off the selvages.

To cut a 4 1/2" square, align the top edge of the ruler against the top of the fabric. Align the 4 1/2" mark on the ruler with the left edge of the fabric. Make a cut.

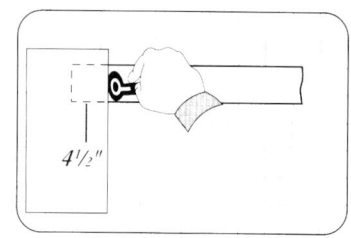

CUTTING THE HALF-SQUARE TRIANGLES

Leave the squares stacked. Place the ruler diagonally across the block, matching the edge of the ruler with both corners. Make a cut.

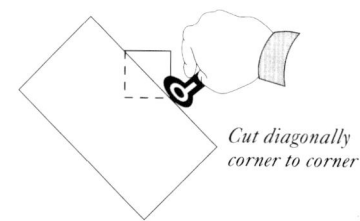
Cut diagonally corner to corner

CUTTING THE QUARTER-SQUARE TRIANGLES

Leave the half-square triangles in place. Lay the ruler diagonally across the block to the opposite corners and make a cut.

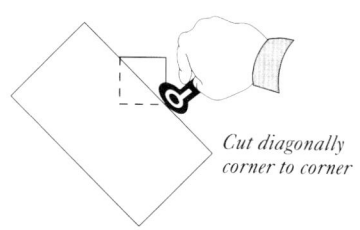
Cut diagonally corner to corner

SEWING TECHNIQUES

A 1/4" seam allowance is ALWAYS used in piecing unless otherwise indicated. It is the most manageable size where several seams meet, and in patchwork there are lots of seams! If you are even a couple of threads off, the problems add up: the block will be too large or too small. It is extremely worthwhile to check your 1/4" seam allowance and be accurate from the very beginning.

SEWING TECHNIQUES, Cont.

To check your 1/4" seam allowance, draw a line on a piece of paper 1/4" away from the cut edge. Place the paper under the presser foot of the sewing machine, with the seam allowance to the right, and bring the needle down through the line that you drew. Release the presser foot. Where the edge of the paper hits on the right is the 1/4" distance. If it isn't on the edge of your presser foot, then mark the line with a piece of masking tape on your sewing machine. This tape edge will act as your seam gauge to ensure an accurate 1/4" seam. Set stitch length at 14 to 16 stitches per inch.

CHAINING

If you are making several blocks, the stitching will go faster if you stitch all of the smaller units together at one time. This is called chaining.

1. Feed pairs of fabric through the sewing machine, one after another, without lifting the presser foot.
2. Remove from the machine and clip the threads between the pairs.

PRESSING

Pressing is very important in any sewing project. In patchwork, the rule is to press both seam allowances toward the darker fabric whenever possible. Where two seams meet, position them so they go in opposite directions. The two seams will nest together when stitched and the points will match. This may mean that one seam isn't pressed toward the darker fabric. The nesting rule applies first.

Use a dry iron when pressing. Press in an up-and-down motion so that the pieces don't become distorted. Press often.

QUILTING

In this booklet, we have included some of our quilting designs and ideas for your personal use and inspiration. You may enlarge the drawings to your desired size using a photocopy machine. Most of the machine quilting that we do is free-motion quilting, without a set pattern.

The term "free-motion" refers to a technique using a darning foot, and dropped feed dogs on your sewing machine, which allows the quilt to move freely under the needle in any direction you guide it. We like to use a clear darning/embroidery foot, because it allows us to see the stitching on the surface of the quilt as it progresses. Aim for an even stitch length that is neither too close together or too far apart. To accomplish this, keep a steady, generous amount of pressure on the foot pedal as you maneuver your quilt through the machine in a slow, even movement. Practice free-motion quilting with a 20" square quilt sandwich (fabric, batting, fabric). Your practice square needs to be large enough that you can move it around freely and sense how it feels when the feed dogs are not controlling the fabric.

You can mark your quilting designs freehand on the quilt or with templates, using a marking tool that washes out.

Petal Play
finished size 42" x 49"

Materials Needed / Cutting Instructions

Materials Needed	Cutting Instructions
A - 1/2 yard large square centers	Cut 3 - 5 1/2" x 42" strips, then cut into 17 - 5 1/2" squares.
B - 1/2 yard large square triangles	Cut 4 - 4 3/8" x 42" strips, then cut into 34 - 4 3/8" squares. Cut these once on the diagonal into half-square triangles.
C - 3/8 yard small square centers	Cut 4 - 3" x 42" strips, then cut into 48 - 3" squares.
D - 5/8 yard small square triangles	Cut 7 - 2 5/8" x 42" strips, then cut into 96 - 2 5/8" squares. Cut these once on the diagonal into half-square triangles.
inner accent 1/4 yard	Cut 5 - 1" x 42" strips, sew together into one long strip, then cut into 2 - 42 1/2" strips for the sides and 2 - 36 1/2" strips for the top
border fabric - 1 1/8 yard OR stripe border - 3 1/4 yards	Cut 2 - 3 1/2" x 43 1/2" lengthwise strips and 2 - 3 1/2" x 42 1/2" lengthwise strips - *OR* - For the stripe border, cut 2 - 8 1/2" x 60" lengths for the sides and 2 - 8 1/2" x 53" lengths for the top and bottom. Be sure to determine if you want the base of the daisies toward the center or the outside of the quilt.
binding - 1/2 yard	
backing - 1 1/2 yards	
quilt batting - 48" x 58"	

Petal Play features the wonderful larger florals, surrounded by coordinating prints. Two border choices are available. In the schematic, we have included a 3" border. Or you could use the 8 1/2" gerber daisy stripe which would change the quilt size to 52" x 59". We have made examples of both.

The center floral squares are two different sizes. Half-square triangles are then cut for the triangles that surround the squares. We have mixed up the triangle colors for even more "Petal Play."

To make this a bed size quilt, make four sets of the piecing and surround it with a border.

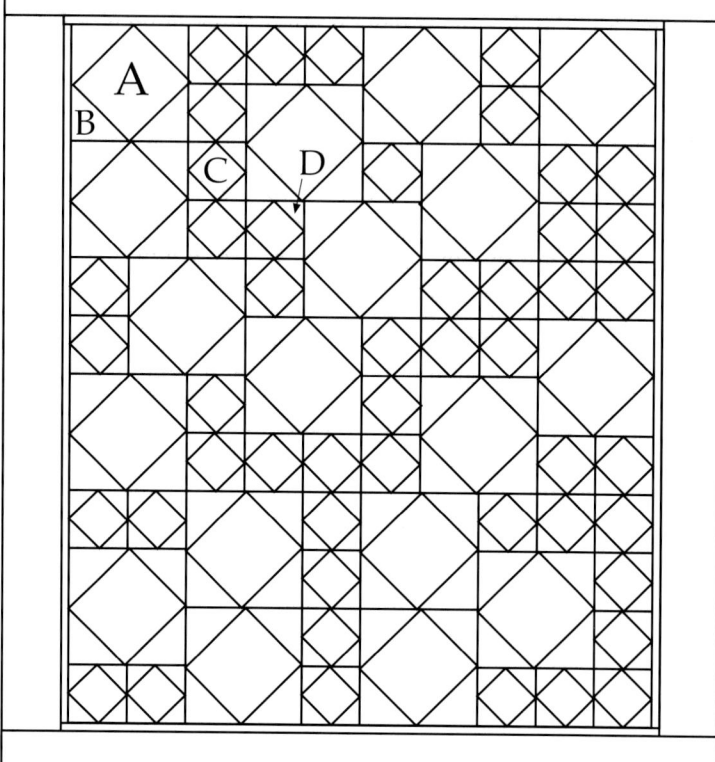

4

Sewing Instructions:

1. Starting with the large squares A, sew a triangle to each of the edges of the square. To line up the points of the triangle with the center of the square, fold the square in half and finger press. Line up the point of the triangle with this line and raw edges even, as shown at right.

Start by sewing the opposite edges first, then press.
Add the other two edges. Make 17.

2. Repeat this step for the smaller center squares C and the triangles. Make 48.

3. Sew the quilt together in sections as shown below. Sew section 1 to section 2.
Sew the little square by itself to section 4, only sewing about 2" starting from the top left-hand corner. Then join section 3 to section 4. Sew the top of section 5 to the bottom of section 3 and little square by itself. Sew section 6 to the right-hand side of this. Finish the seam of the little square and sew section 6 onto the bottom of section 4. Sew this large unit to the section 1 & section 2 unit. Add this to section 7.

4. For the border accent, fold the 1" strips in half, wrong sides together. Sew the two side strips on first, lining up raw edges. Sew on the top and bottom strips, overlapping at the corners.

5. For the 3" border, sew two of the 43 1/2" border strips to the sides of the quilt, then sew the other two 42 1/2" strips to the top and bottom of the quilt. Press toward the border strips. For the stripe border option, follow the instructions for mitering corners as per the Tablecloth, page 22.

6. Layer the quilt.
We quilted large daisy shapes over the pieced area with variegated thread which gives a playful look and repeats the theme. In the stripe border we outline quilted the daisies and leaves. See below.

7. Bind the quilt.

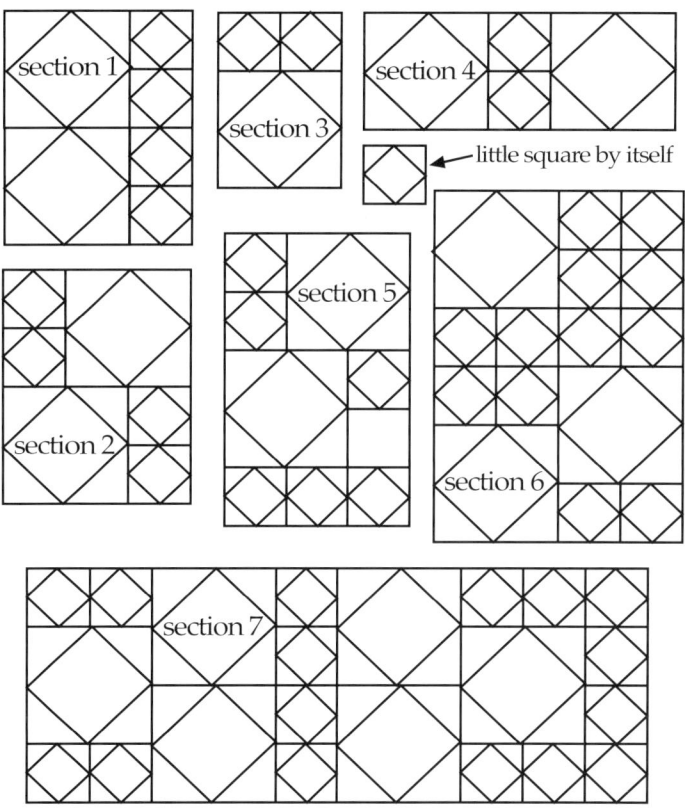

daisy quilting

Lazy Logs

*finished sizes: crib - 33 3/4" x 47 41/4," lap - 60 3/4" x 74 1/4,"
double - 81" x 87 3/4," queen - 87 3/4" x 94 1/2"*

This mock log cabin has strips added to two sides of the center block. Pre-cut strips are used to assure accurate size blocks. Cutting Instructions are given on the chart below.

Materials Needed and Cutting Instructions

	Crib	Lap	Double	Queen
A - orange 3 1/2" x 3 1/2"	**1/3 yard** Cut 3 - 3 1/2"x 42" strips, then cut into 35 - 3 1/2" squares	**1 yard** Cut 9 - 3 1/2"x 42" strips, then cut into 99 - 3 1/2" squares	**1 1/3 yards** Cut 13 - 3 1/2" x 42" strips, then cut into 156 - 3 1/2" squares	**1 5/8 yards** Cut 16 - 3 1/2" x 42" strips, then cut into 182 - 3 1/2" squares
B - orange 1 1/4" x 3 1/2"	**1/8 yard** cut 3 strips	**3/8 yard** cut 9 strips	**1/2 yard** cut 13 strips	**5/8 yard** cut 16 strips
C - purple 1 1/4" x 4 1/4"	**1/4 yard** cut 4 strips	**1/2 yard** cut 11 strips	**3/4 yard** cut 18 strips	**7/8 yard** cut 21 strips
D - orange 1 1/4" x 4 1/4"	**1/4 yard** cut 4 strips	**1/2 yard** cut 11 strips	**3/4 yard** cut 18 strips	**7/8 yard** cut 21 strips
E - purple 1 1/4" x 5"	**1/4 yard** cut 5 strips	**1/2 yard** cut 13 strips	**3/4 yard** cut 20 strips	**7/8 yard** cut 23 strips
F - orange 1 1/4" x 5"	**1/4 yard** cut 5 strips	**1/2 yard** cut 13 strips	**3/4 yard** cut 20 strips	**7/8 yard** cut 23 strips
G - purple 1 1/4" x 5 3/4"	**1/4 yard** cut 5 strips	**5/8 yard** cut 15 strips	**7/8 yard** cut 23 strips	**1 yard** cut 26 strips
H - orange 1 1/4" x 5 3/4"	**1/4 yard** cut 5 strips	**5/8 yard** cut 15 strips	**7/8 yard** cut 23 strips	**1 yard** cut 26 strips
I - purple 1 1/4" x 6 1/2"	**1/4 yard** cut 7 strips	**2/3 yard** cut 17 strips	**1 yard** cut 26 strips	**1 1/8 yard** cut 31 strips
J - orange 1 1/4" x 6 1/2"	**1/4 yard** cut 7 strips	**2/3 yard** cut 17 strips	**1 yard** cut 26 strips	**1 1/8 yard** cut 31 strips
K - purple 1 1/4" x 7 1/4	**1/4 yard** cut 7 strips	**3/4 yard** cut 20 strips	**1 1/8 yard** cut 31 strips	**1 3/8 yard** cut 37 strips
binding	**3/8 yard**	**1/2 yard**	**1/2 yard**	**2/3 yard**
backing	**1 1/2 yard**	**4 yards**	**5 1/8 yards**	**8 1/2 yards**
quilt batting	**40" x 54"**	**66" x 80"**	**88" x 94"**	**94" x 100"**

Sewing Instructions

1. Make several blocks at one time, chaining them together., as shown in fig. 1. Cut apart and press.

2. Add C to AB as shown in fig. 2 in the same manner. Press toward C.

3. Continue the process of adding the strips, always pressing toward the outer strip. Unfinished size of the completed block is 7 1/4". (Finished size of the block is 6 3/4")

4. Arrange the blocks in rows as shown on the schematic below. Sew together in horizontal rows, then sew row 1 to row 2, etc.

5. Layer the quilt. We quilted a swirl pattern in the diagonal rows created by the alternating colors.

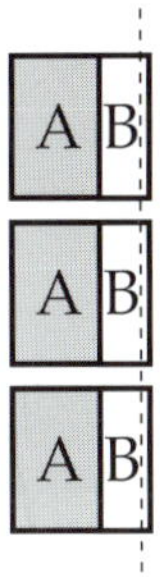

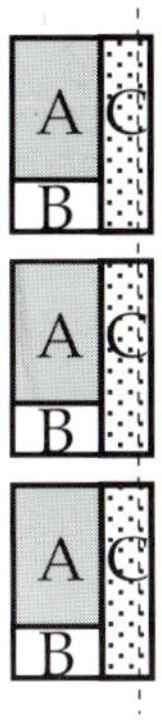

6. Bind the quilt.

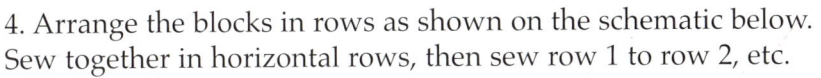

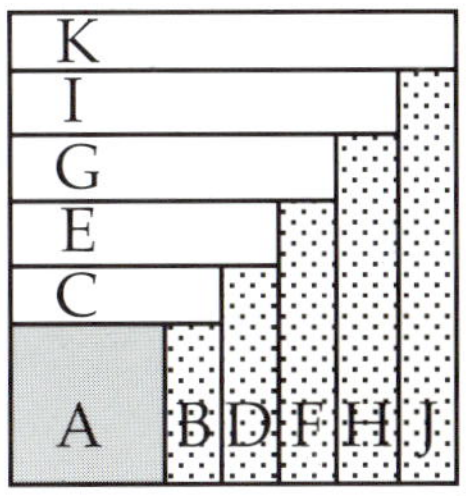

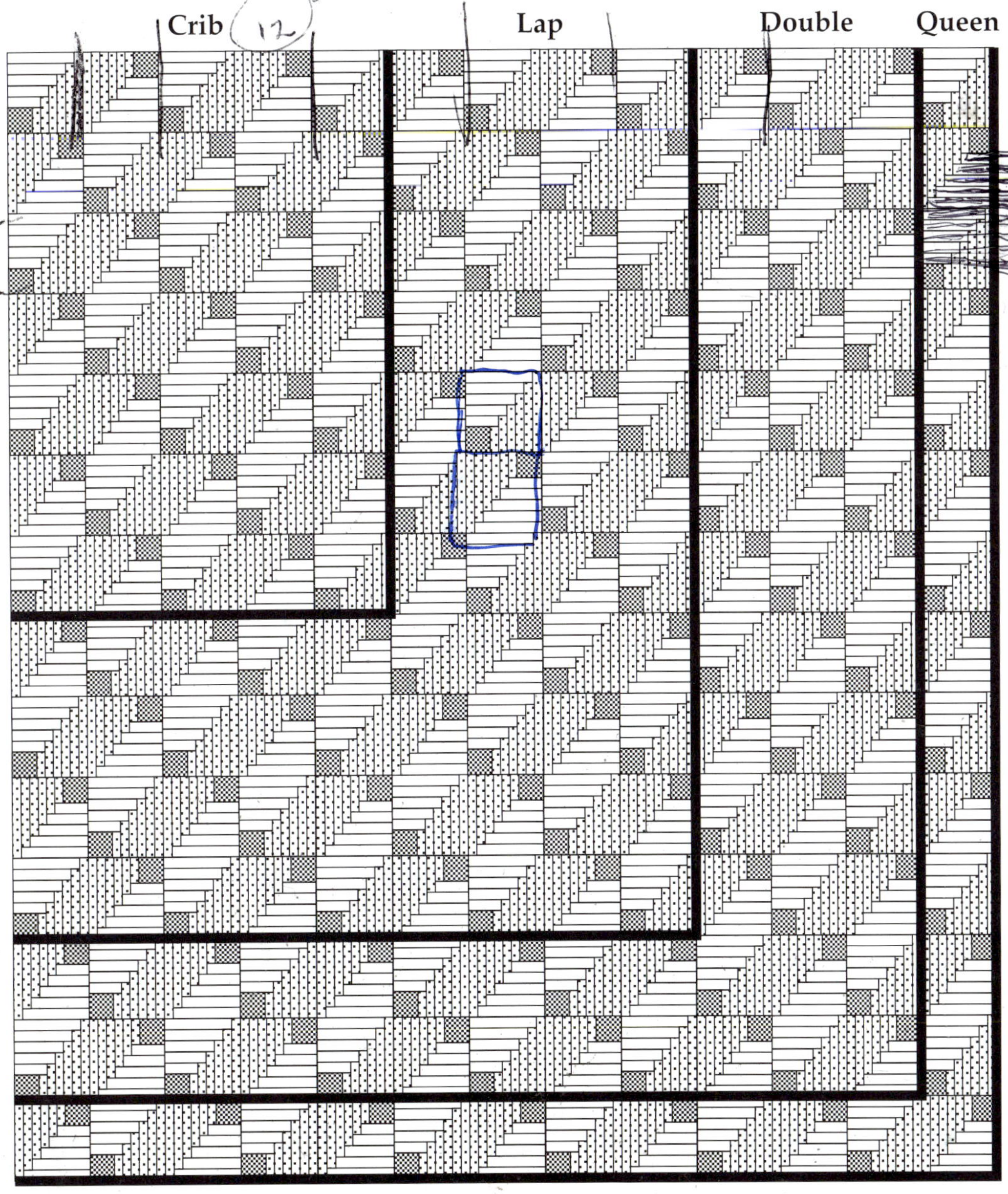

Market Day Tote
finished size 16" x 12 1/2," with a 3" gusset

Materials Needed / Cutting Instructions

Materials Needed	Cutting Instructions
center section 2 - 7" x 10" rectangles	B - cut 2 - 6 1/2" x 9 1/2"
center section 1 - 7" x 8" rectangle	C - cut 1 - 6 1/2" x 7 1/2"
side panels 1/3 yard	A - cut 2 - 5 1/2" x 25 1/2"
handles 1/4 yard or 8" x 26"	Cut 2 - 3 1/2" x 25"
lining 1/2 yard	Cut 1 - 16 1/2" x 25 1/2"
22" x 28" thin batting for the handles and body of tote	Cut 1 - 16 1/2" x 25 1/2" rectangle for the body of the bag and 2 - 1 1/2" x 25" rectangles for the handles
optional pocket two 7" x 8" rectangles	Cut 2 - 6 1/2" x 7 1/2" rectangles

Medium size tote bags are so handy to take shopping, or to carry your latest quilting project when you go to quilt group or on vacation. For this tote, we featured a large single gerber daisy cut from the Maraposa border stripe. The side panels are a coordinate from the collection. The handles are cut from the main print stripe left over from one of the quilts.

(finished measurements shown)

Sewing Instructions:
Refer to schematic at left.

1. Sew B to each side of C. Press seams toward C. Add A to each side of the center panel. Press seams toward A.

2. Fold right sides of the bag together and stitch sides. With the wrong sides out, fold the bottom corner of the bag on top of the side seam. Measure down the angle 2 1/2" on each side, mark with a pencil or pin. Stitch across from edge to edge. This makes the gusset. Repeat for the other side of the bag. See fig. 1

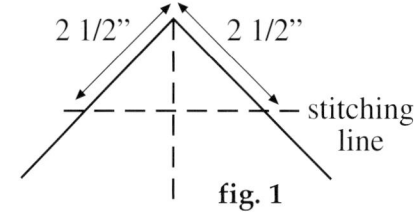

3. Optional pocket--place two squares of fabric right sides together. Stitch around the edges leaving a small area open to turn. Trim the corners, turn to the right side, and press the edges. Center the pocket 1 1/2" from the top edge of the lining having the edge with the pressed under opening at the bottom of the pocket. Topstitch around the sides and bottom of the pocket. See fig. 2

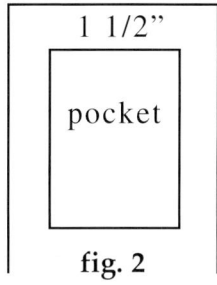

4. Place the batting on the lining. Place right sides of the lining together and stitch the side seams through the batting and lining. Make the gussets in the lining as you did in step 2. See fig. 1

5. Press the edges under 1/4" on the long edges of the handles. Fold the handles in half vertically, matching up the folded under edges and press. Open the handles and insert a piece of batting under the 1/4" edge, lining it up with the center fold. Pull the remaining fabric over the batting and pin the edges and batting together. Top stitch 1/8" from both vertical edges. See fig. 3

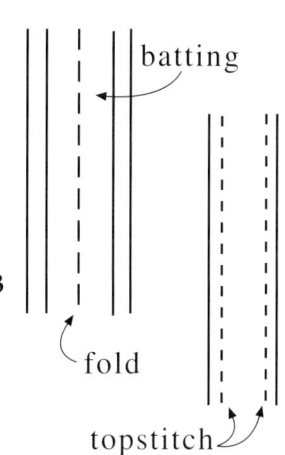

6. Turn under the top edges of the batting and lining 1/4" and press.

7. Place the handles on outside of the bag as shown in fig. 4. Topstitch 1/4" from the edge. Repeat for other side of the bag.

8. Insert the lining in the bag pushing it into the corners. Match up the top edges and topstitch 1/8" from the edge and again 1/4" from the edge.

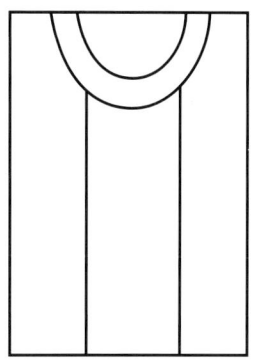

Pinwheels in the Garden
finished size 48" x 56"

Materials Needed / Cutting Instructions

Materials Needed	Cutting Instructions
Panel - 1 yard stripe	Trim panel to 33 1/2" x 42 1/2"
1st border 1/4 yard	Cut 2 - 2" x 42 1/2" strips for sides Cut 2 - 1 1/2" x 36 1/2" strips for top and bottom
2nd border 1/2 yard each of two different lights, 1/2 yard of two different darks	Cut 4 - 2 7/8" x 42" strips from the two lights Cut 4 - 2 7/8" x 42" strips from the two darks Then cut all the strips into 2 7/8" squares. You need 88 light and 88 dark squares. Cut these squares once on the diagonal into half-square triangles (these are the cutting instructions for the 44 pinwheels)
3rd border and binding 1 yard	Cut 5 - 2 1/2" x 42" strips. Sew together into one long strip. From this long strip cut 2 - 2 1/2" x 52 1/2" for the sides. Cut 2 - 2 1/2" x 48 1/2" for the top and bottom.
backing - 3 yards	
quilt batting - 54" x 62"	

The beautiful gerber daisy stripe panel is the feature fabric in this quilt. It is then surrounded by three borders, one of which is pieced pinwheels.

Sewing Instructions

1. Sew the first border to the panel, starting with the sides, then add top and bottom borders. Press toward the panel.

2. There are two darks and two lights for the pinwheels. From these make four different combinations. Arrange the half-square triangles as shown in fig. 1. Sew units as shown to make 44 pinwheel blocks.

fig. 1

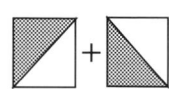
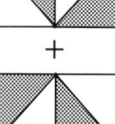
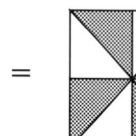
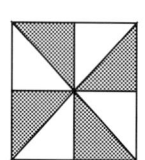

3. Sew eleven pinwheel blocks together for each side and stitch to the quilt. Press toward the first border. Sew eleven pinwheel blocks together for the top and bottom and stitch to the quilt. Press toward the first border.

4. For the third border, sew the side borders on first, then add the top and bottom. Press toward the third border.

5. Layer the quilt. We outline quilted the images in the panel to make them stand out. Following the diagonal lines on the pinwheels, quilt through all the borders as shown in fig. 2.

6. Bind the quilt.

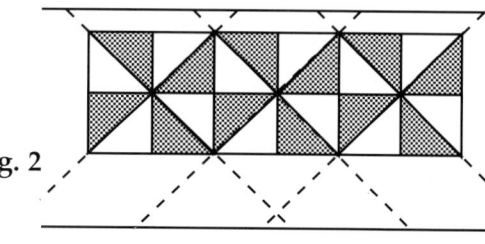

fig. 2

Hidden Treasures
finished size 42" x 60"

This quilt was inspired by Frank Lloyd Wright's amazing stained-glass windows. In the square spaces, simple pieced blocks were inserted. The play of colors and pattern using the Maraposa fabric creates a garden scene. This quilt could easily be made longer by adding inches to the strips and wider by adding more of the strips and blocks. The wall hanging size can also be used as a lap quilt.

We used the vineyard palette for this quilt, letting the multi colored daisy speak as the theme print, with the red dahlia as a support. Deep dark tones were added for definition, bright tones for sparkle, and mediums to fill in. The patterns in the fabrics add texture and interest. When designing the quilt, we cut the vertical strips first, then made the blocks choosing the colors to work with the strips.

Materials Needed:
  1/2 yard multi-color daisy
  1/4 yard red dahlia
Darks
  3/4 yard dark red bud
  (for piecing and binding)
  1/3 yard deep green dandelion
  1/3 yard purple dahlia
  1/4 yard deep rose daisy
Brights
  1/4 yard gold daisy
  1/4 yard yellow gold tile
  1/4 yard lavender dandelion
Mediums
  1/4 yard peach tile
  1/2 yard green tile
  1/4 yard peach daisy
Backing
  1 7/8 yard
Batting
  48" x 66"

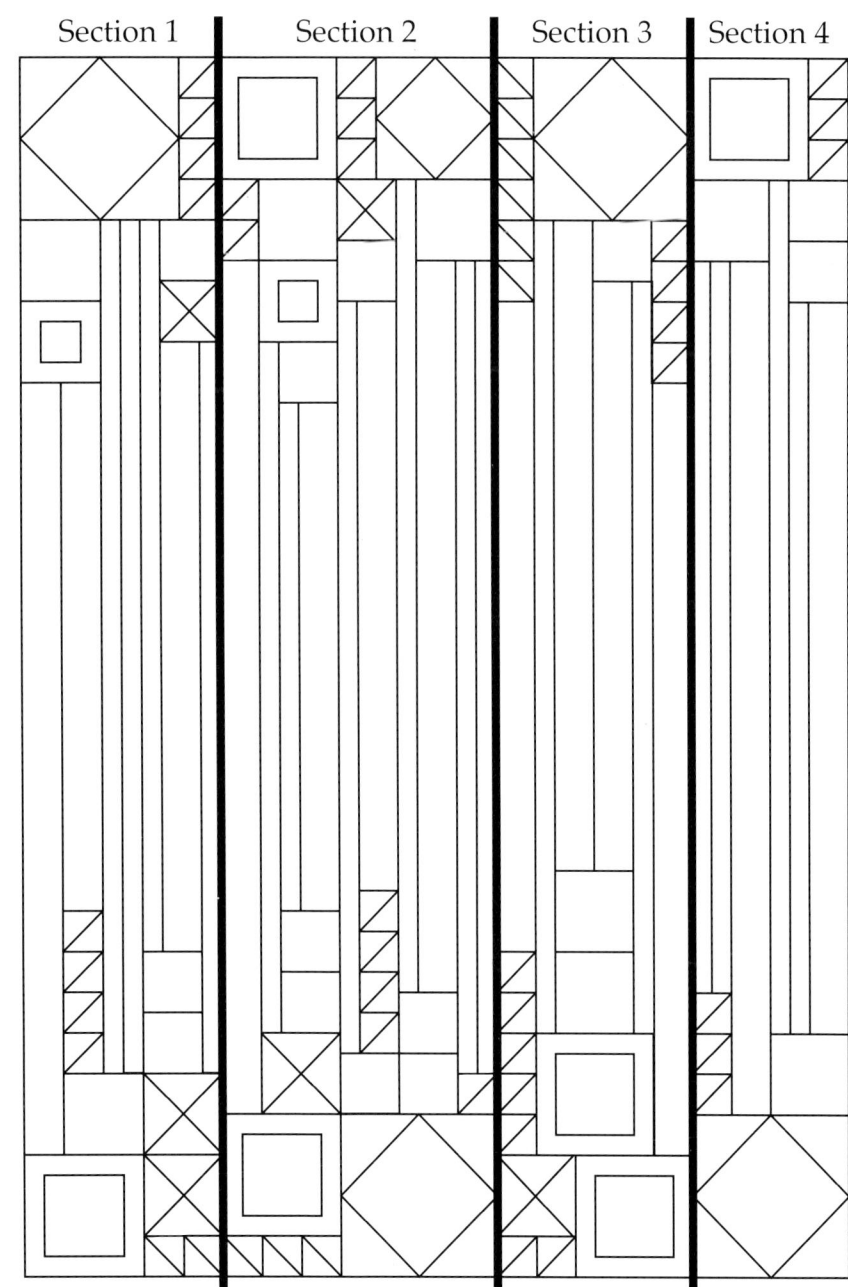

Cutting and Sewing Instructions for Pieced Blocks
Instructions are given for each of the pieced units. Refer to the quilt photo for placement of fabrics.

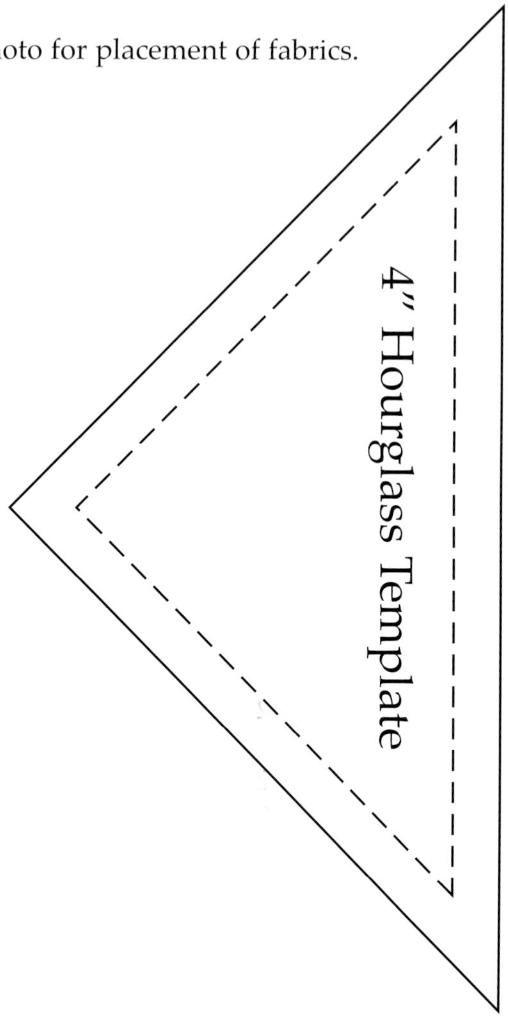

8" square on point
4 are needed
A - 6 1/4" x 6 1/4"
B - cut 2 - 4 7/8" squares, then cut once on the diagonal into half-square triangles

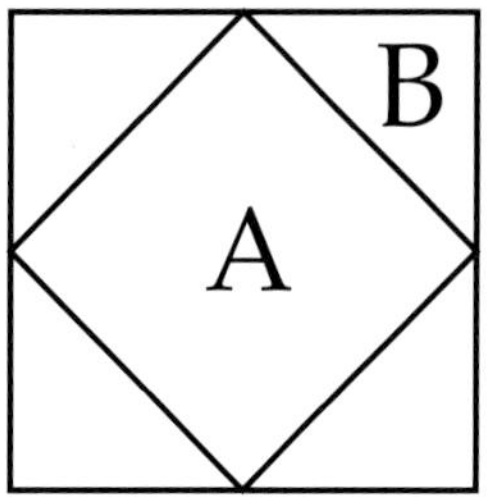

6" square on point
1 is needed
A - 4 3/4" x 4 3/4"
B - cut 2 - 3 7/8" squares, then cut once on the diagonal into half-square triangles

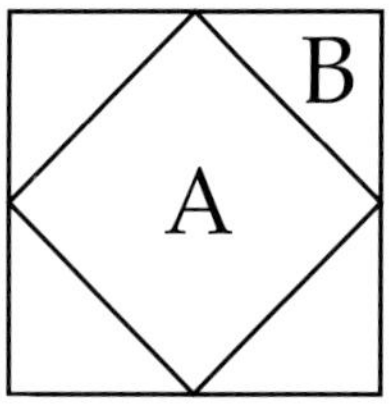

6" bordered square
6 are needed
A - 4 1/2" x 4 1/2"
B - 1 1/2" x 4 1/2"
C - 1 1/2" x 5 1/2"
D - 1 1/2" x 5 1/2"
E - 1 1/2" x 6 1/2"

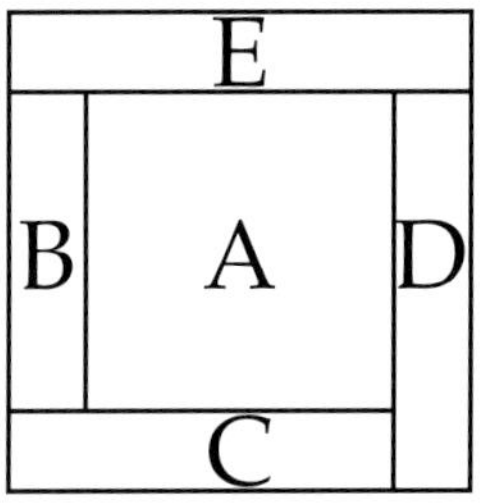

4" bordered square
2 are needed
A - 2 1/2" x 2 1/2"
B - 1 1/2" x 2 1/2"
C - 1 1/2" x 3 1/2"
D - 1 1/2" x 3 1/2"
E - 1 1/2" x 4 1/2"

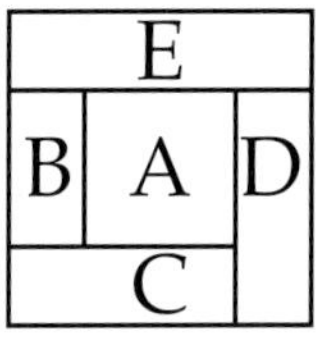

4" hourglass
4 are needed
Using the template provided, cut two each from two different fabrics.

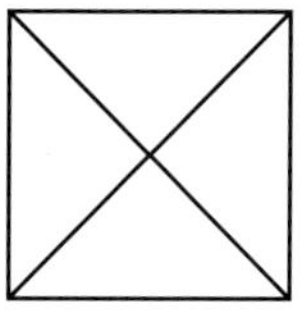

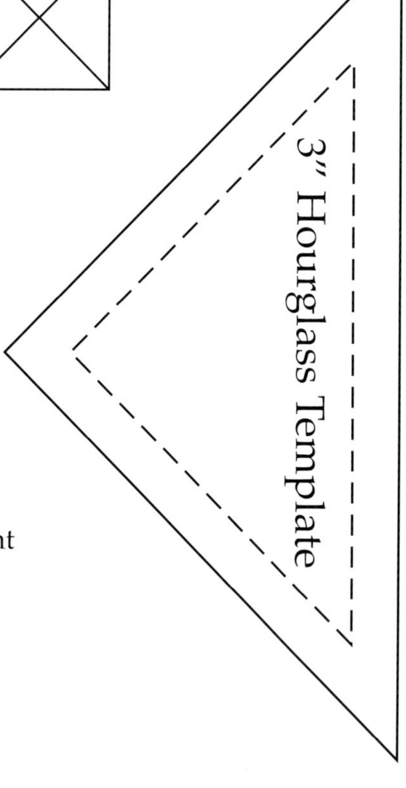

3" hourglass
2 are needed
Using the template provided, cut two each from two different fabrics

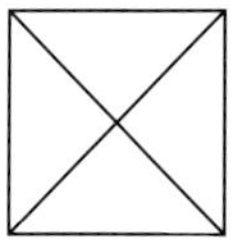

2" half square triangles
46 are needed
Cut these as you come to them when laying out the design.
Cut a 2 7/8" square from two different fabrics, cut once on the diagonal into half-square triangles.

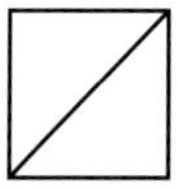

Cut 6 - 4 1/2" squares and 8 - 3 1/2" squares from multi-colored daisy print

Cut 2 - 4 1/2" square and 5 - 3 1/2" squares from red dahlia print

Cutting Instructions, continued.
Refer to the photograph for the fabric placement.

Section 1 strips
1 - 2 1/2" x 38 1/2"
2 - 2 1/2" x 26 1/2"
3 - 1 1/2" x 42 1/2"
4 - 1 1/2" x 42 1/2"
5 - 1 1/2" x 36 1/2"
6 - 2 1/2" x 30 1/2"
7 - 1 1/2" x 36 1/2"

Section 2 strips
8 - 2 1/2" x 42 1/2"
9 - 1 1/2" x 34 1/2"
10 - 1 1/2" x 25 1/2"
11 - 2 1/2" x 25 1/2"
12 - 1 1/2" x 37 1/2"
13 - 2 1/2" x 29 1/2"
14 - 1 1/2" x 40 1/2"
15 - 2 1/2" x 36 1/2"
16 - 1 1/2" x 40 1/2"
17 - 1 1/2" x 40 1/2"

Section 3 strips
18 - 2 1/2" x 32 1/2"
19 - 1 1/2" x 40 1/2"
20 - 2 1/2" x 32 1/2"
21 - 2 1/2" x 29 1/2"
22 - 1 1/2" x 37 1/2"
23 - 2 1/2" x 38 1/2"

Section 4 strips
24 - 1 1/2" x 36 1/2"
25 - 1 1/2" x 36 1/2"
26 - 2 1/2" x 42 1/2"
27 - 1 1/2" x 42 1/2"
28 - 1 1/2" x 36 1/2"
29 - 2 1/2" x 36 1/2"

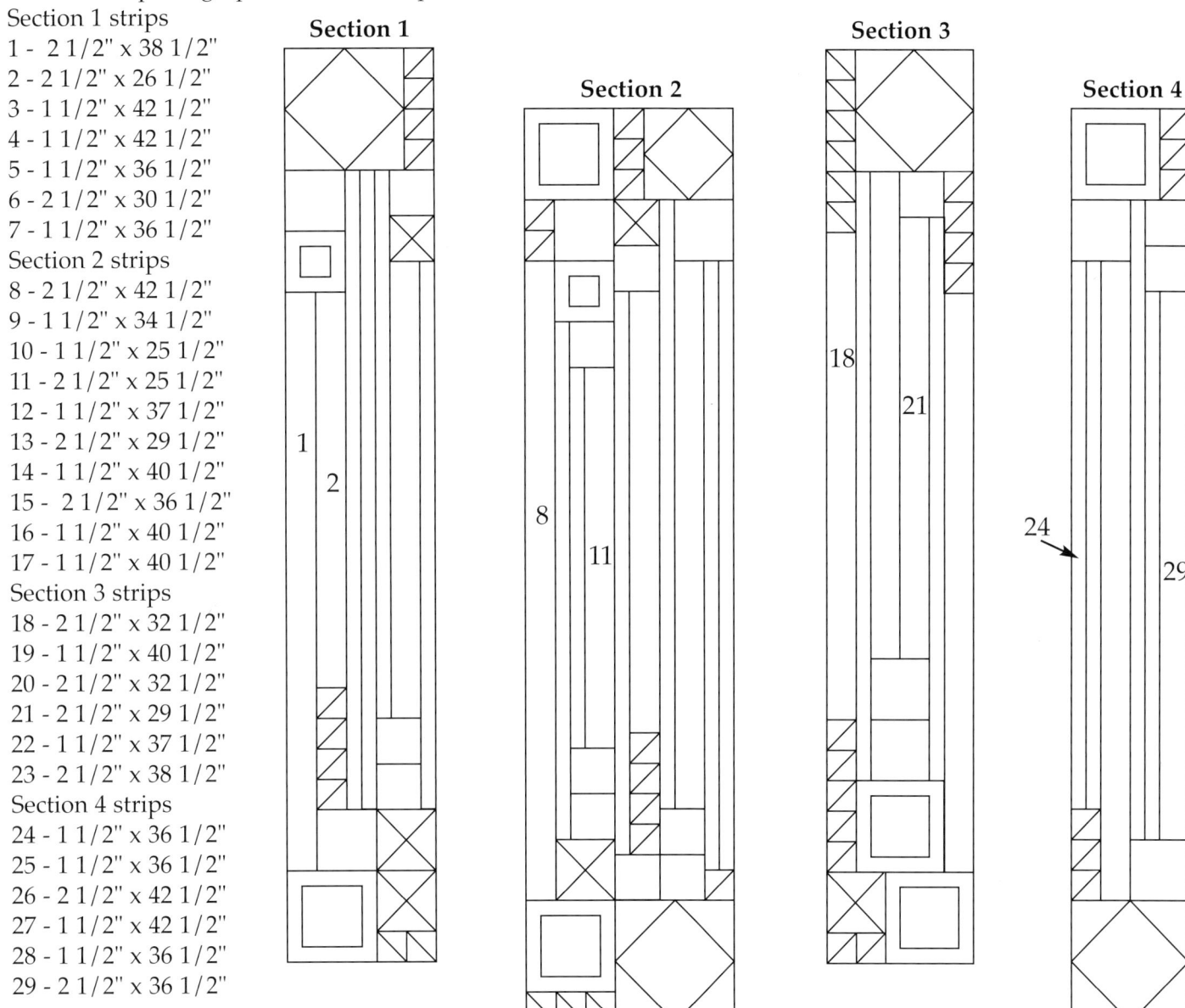

Sewing Instructions:
1. Start by cutting the vertical strips for the quilt and place them on a design wall or table to make sure you like the color arrangement. Then begin with the 8" bordered square blocks.
Continue making the pieced blocks until they all are completed.
Schematics are included for the simple piecing of each block.

2. The quilt is pieced in sections, from left to right, as you can see in the quilt schematic above. (The strips are numbered in numerical sequence, starting with number 1 on the far left of Section 1.)
There are times where you stitch part of a seam, join another seam, and come back and finish the first seam.
Once the sections are finished, join them together.

3. Layer the quilt. We quilted vines with leaves coming up the vertical strips.
The blocks are stitched more traditionally.

4. Bind the quilt.

Victoria's Garden
finished size 80" x 80"

In Victoria's Garden, the center garden patch is surrounded by the gerber daisy border print. The border squares are just one inch larger than the center garden patch squares. Multi-colored daisy fabric patches are scattered among the squares to create a daisy garden theme. This quilt design is very adaptable to a variety of bed sizes. If you want to make it larger, add more squares to the outside edge. For a baby quilt, leave off the outside border squares.

Materials Needed / Cutting Instructions

Materials Needed	Cutting Instructions
border — 3 1/4 yard border print	Cut the border print apart measuring from the outside of each scroll with the gerber daisies in the middle. This measurement needs to be 10 1/2" x 56 1/2". Cut 4.
center 3 1/2" squares and outside border 4 1/2" squares — 1 yard multi-colored daisy print — 2/3 yard yellow fern print — leftover dahlia print (from the border print above) — leftover fern-scroll print (from the border print above) — 1/4 yard each of ten other prints	For the center squares you need 144 - 3 1/2" squares. We used approximately 28 of the multicolored gerber daisies, 20 dahlia (cut from the leftover border print), 16 of the fern print, and cut the rest from the other prints. For the outside border you will need 204 - 4 1/2" squares. We used approximately 40 multi-colored gerber daisies, 15 dahlia (cut from the leftover border print), 20 fern prints, and twenty fern-scrolls. To make the fern-scrolls, cut the 2 1/2" x 56 1/2" strip of the fern-scroll stripe in half lengthwise into two 28 1/4" strips. Sew the long sides together to form one 4 1/2" x 28 1/4" strip. Cut into 4 1/2" squares. The remaining squares are cut from the other prints.
5/8 yard for binding	
5 yards for backing	
86" x 86" batting	

Cutting instructions for the border print: Cut off selvage

Cut the daisy stripe 10 1/2" from below the selvage to just below the large swirl stripe.

Cut the dahlia stripe 3 1/2" from below the large swirl stripe to the bottom of the dahlias, just above the thin scroll stripe.

Cut the fern-scroll stripe 2 1/2" from above the thin scroll stripe to the bottom of the ferns, just above the next thin scroll stripe.

Continue the process for the next repeat. The bottom repeat will be left over for placemats, etc.

(The stripe only has three repeats so it is necessary to purchase two lengths. Part of the leftover fabric is used in the piecing. There are several other projects in the book that make use of the border stripe, including the placemats, tote bag, and pillow shams.)

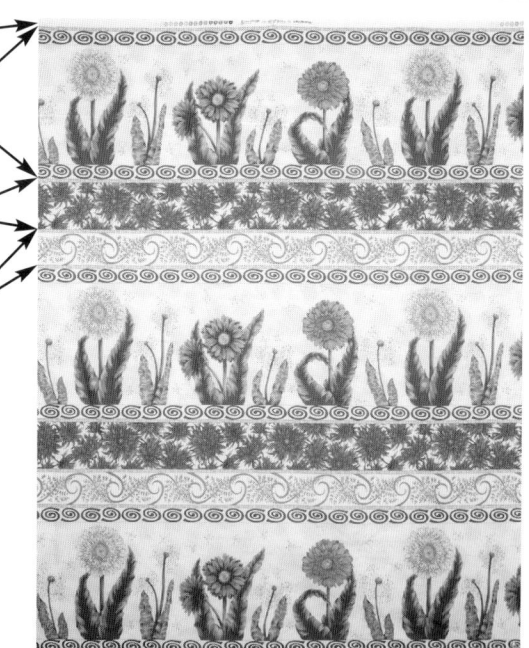

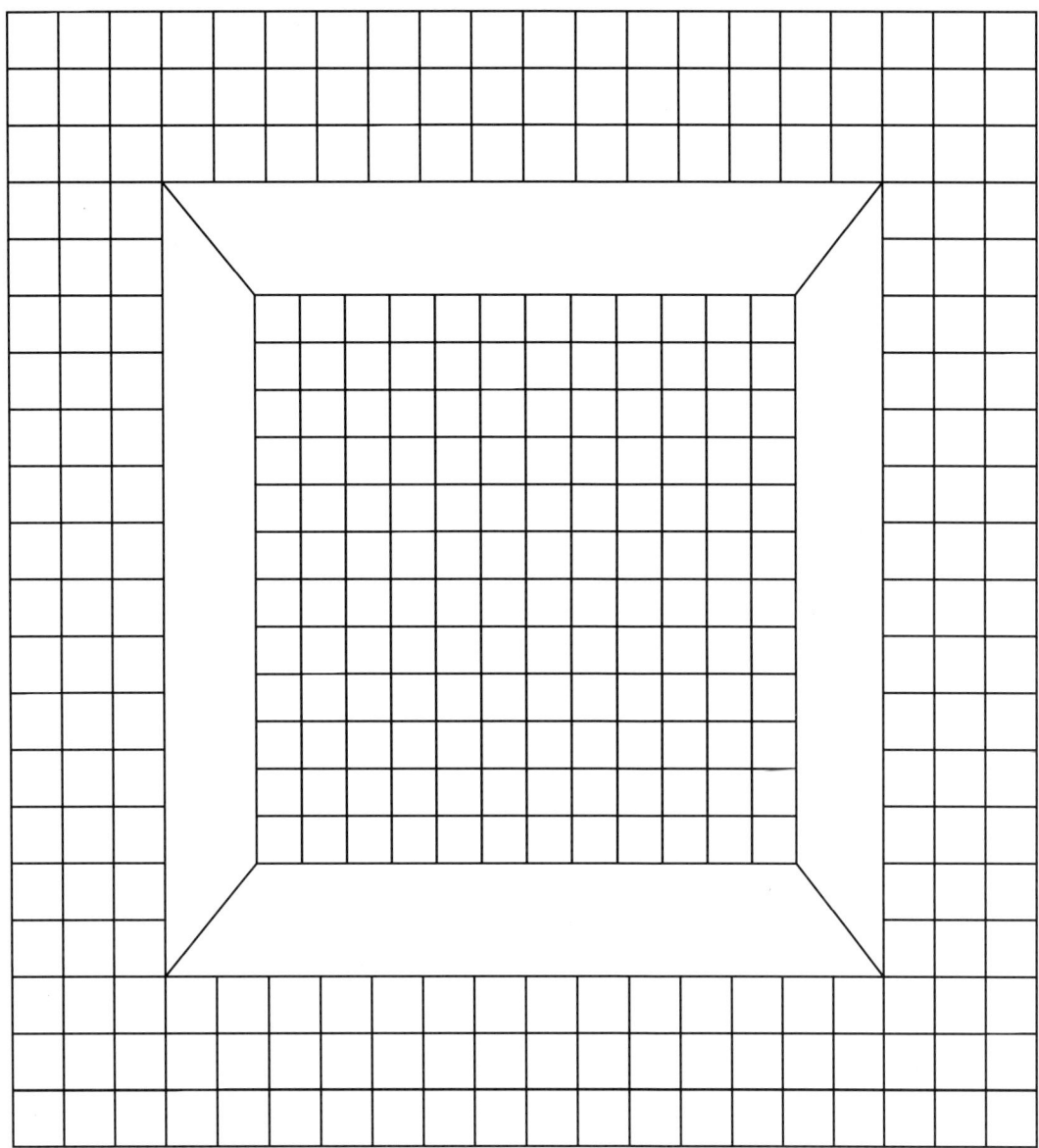

Sewing Instructions:

1. Arrange the center squares in twelve rows of twelve each. Sew together in rows, then join row 1 to row 2, etc.

2. Fold the border strips in half and place a pin at the center mark. Match the pin to the center of each side of the center section. Decide if you want the flowers of the border strips to face to the center of the quilt or the outside of the quilt before pinning. Follow the tablecloth instructions on page 22 for making mitered corners.

3. Arrange the side 4 1/2" squares in three rows of fourteen each. Arrange the top and bottom rows of squares in three rows of twenty each. Sew together and add the sides, then the top and bottom borders.

4. Layer the quilt top. To quilt the top, stitch diagonally through the squares in both directions. Outline stitch the daisies in the border. Then fill in the background by echo quilting beyond the flowers in flower shapes.

Petal Play Pillow
finished size 18" x 18"

Four large *Petal Play* blocks were put together with sashing to make this colorful 18" pillow.

Materials Needed:

Refer to schematic for placement.
Scraps from the Petal Play Quilt can be used for the blocks.

1/4 yard for A

4 1/2" x 4 1/2" of eight different fabrics for B or four different fabrics if you keep B the same around A

1/2 yard for sashing and backing

18" pillow form

optional - batting for the pillow top if you want to quilt it.

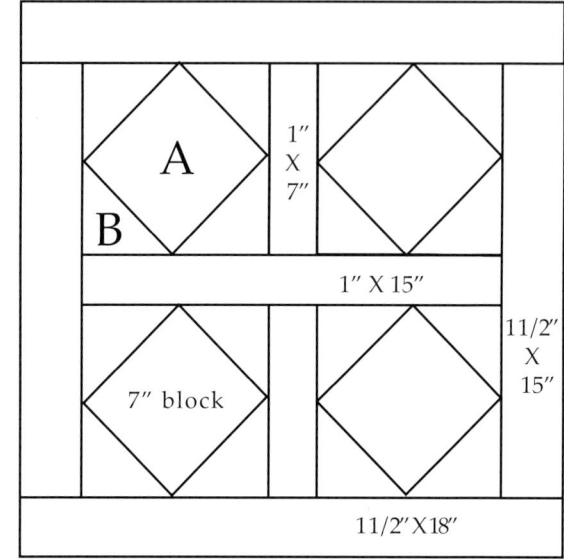

(finished measurements shown)

Cutting:

A - cut 4 - 5 1/2" squares
B - from each of the eight fabrics cut a 4 3/8" square, then cut each square once on the diagonal into half-square triangles.

From the backing and sashing fabric cut 2 - 18 1/2" x 12" rectangles.

From the leftovers cut the following:
2 - 2" x 18 1/2" rectangles, 2 - 2" x 15 1/2" rectangles,
1 - 1 1/2" x 15 1/2" rectangle, and 2 - 1 1/2" x 7 1/2" rectangles.

Sewing Instructions:

1. Construct four Petal Play blocks following the instructions on page 5.

2. Refer to the schematic and insert the sashing between the blocks. Sew together as shown in. fig. 1.

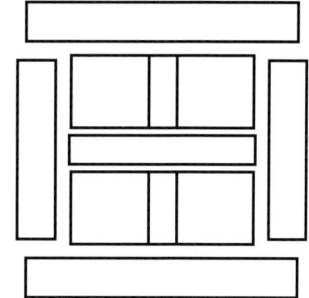

fig. 1

3. On the backing, turn under one raw edge 1/4" on the 18 1/2" side of each rectangle and sew.

4. Quilt the pillow top if desired.

5. Place the right side of the backing on the right side of the top of the pillow matching up the outside edges. The hemmed edges will overlap in the center creating a pocket on the back where the pillow form will be inserted. See fig. 2

Stitch around the edges 1/4" from the edge.
Trim the corners.
Turn to the right side and insert pillow form.

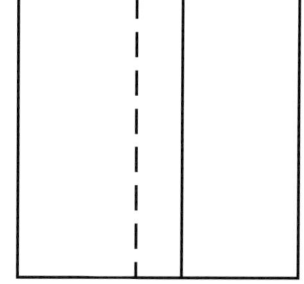

fig. 2

Victoria's Garden Pillow
finished size 16" x 16"

Sixteen three inch squares were stitched together for the pillow center, Every other square is the large daisy theme print. Other bright squares in a variety of colors and prints are inserted between the daisy squares, and the yellow and green fern print borders the bright center.

Materials Needed:
1/8 yard large daisy print
eight different 3 1/2" squares of other brights
2/3 yard border and backing
16" pillow form

Cutting Instructions:
Cut 8 daisy and 8 bright 3 1/2" squares
Cut 2 - 2 1/2" x 12 1/2" rectangles for the side borders
Cut 2 - 2 1/2" x 16 1/2" rectangles for the top and bottom borders
From the backing fabric, cut 2 - 16 1/2" x 11" rectangles

Sewing Instructions:
1. Arrange the squares -- daisy-bright-daisy-bright, etc. Refer to the photograph.
Sew the squares together in rows, then sew row 1 to row 2, etc.

2. Add the side borders, then the top and bottom borders. Press.

3. On the backing, turn under one raw edge 1/4" on the 16 1/2" side of each rectangle and sew. (Refer to instructions for the Petal Play Pillow on the opposite page.)

4. Place the right side of the backing on the right side of the top of the pillow top. The back two sections will overlap. This creates an envelope to insert the pillow form. Stitch around the four sides of the pillow. Trim the corners. Turn to the right side and insert the pillow form.

Pillow Sham
finished size 19" x 27"

Matching pillow shams add a nice finish to a bed quilt. We used the leftover stripe fabric from the Victoria's Garden quilt plus another strip of fabric to get the desired width. Be sure to measure your pillow before you begin, as pillows vary in size.

Materials Needed for 1 Sham:
2/3 yard or a combination of fabrics to equal this amount
1 yard for backing

Cutting and Sewing Instructions
1. Measure your pillow to get the correct size, adding 1/2" in both length and width.

2. Sew the stripe and the other fabric strip together, making the piece the same measurement as the pillow measurement recorded in #1.

3. Cut two backing pieces 19 1/2" x 16 1/2". You may need to adjust these measurements to the size of your pillow. Sew these two sections as per the backing instructions for the Petal Play pillow on the opposite page.

Tablecloth
finished size 55" x 55"

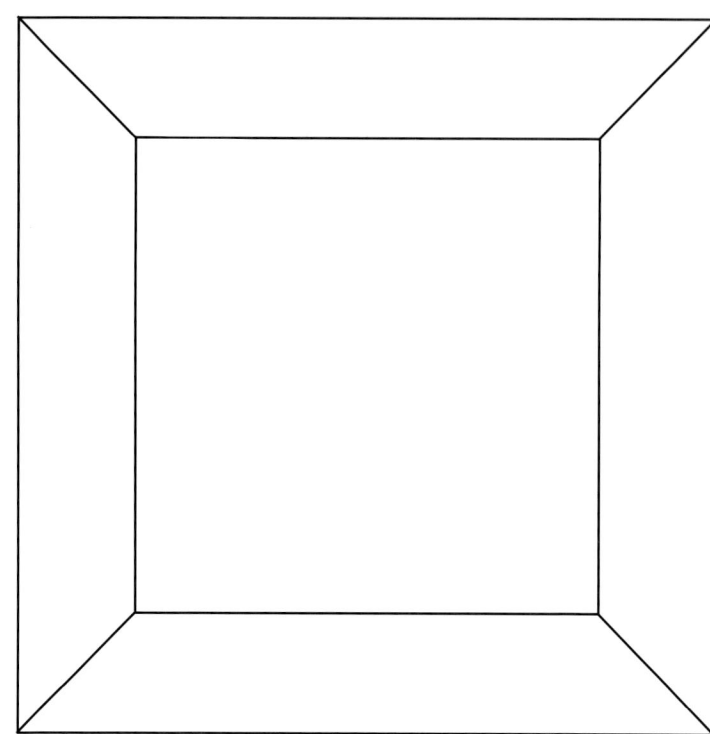

The Maraposa Tablecloth consists of a center print with a border on all four sides. The theme stripe is repeated three times in the 42" width of fabric. To make the tablecloth it is necessary to purchase two lengths of fabric. With the remaining fabric, you can make six placemats and four napkins. Or you could use the fabric in another project.

Materials Needed:
3 yards of stripe
1 1/4 yard center of tablecloth (daisy print)
2 1/3 yard backing

Cutting:
Cut a 39 1/2" square from the center fabric.
Cut 4 - 8 1/2" x 55 1/2" lengths from the stripe featuring the daisy.
Cut one piece of backing fabric 55 1/2" in length. Cut the remaining backing fabric into two 14" wide strips. Stitch these to each selvage edge of the 55 1/2" piece to make one 55 1/2" x 55 1/2" square.

Sewing Instructions:
1. Measure in 8 1/4" from both ends of the 55 1/2" stripe. Pin this to the right side of the center fabric 1/4" in from the raw edge. Pin along the edge to the other end and place another pin 1/4" in from the edge of the fabric. Sew between the pins. Repeat on all four sides. See fig. 1

2. To form the mitered corner, take tablecloth to the ironing board. (See fig. 2.) On the corner, fold under the top fabric as shown at a forty five degree angle. Press. Lift up the top edge and pin the two border fabrics together. Stitch on the fold line from the inside of the quilt out. Trim the seam allowance to 1/4". Repeat for all four sides.

3. Place the right side of the backing on the right side of the tablecloth. Sew around the edges leaving an opening to turn the cloth to the right side. Turn and press edges. Sew the opening shut.

4. Topstitch 1/4" in from the finished edge and on the edge of where the border and center section meet. This will secure the backing to the tablecloth.

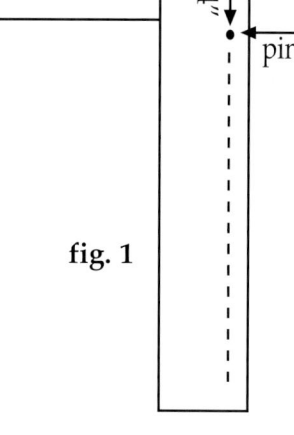

fig. 1

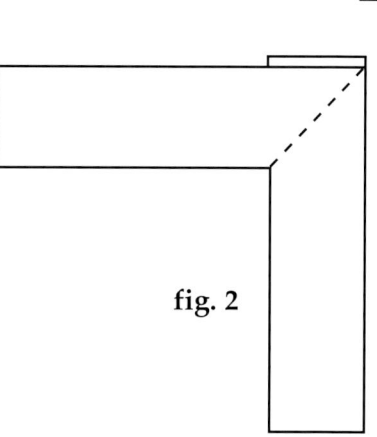

fig. 2

22

Placemats
finished size 13" x 18"

You can back these simple placemats with a coordinating fabric, or you can insert a very thin batting for a quilted look. Your placemats can even be reversible if you desire, depending on your choice of backing fabrics.

Materials Needed:
We used some of the leftover border stripe fabric. (If you are purchasing fabric and not using a stripe you can get two placemats out of 3/8 yard.) You will also need to purchase fabric for the backing. If you place the placemats lengthwise on the fabric you can get six backings out of 1 1/4 yard. Batting is optional.

Cutting Instructions:
Cut placemats and backing 13 1/2" x 18 1/2"

Sewing Instructions:
1. Place right sides of placemat and backing together. (If batting is desired, place these fabrics on the batting.) Stitch around the four sides leaving an opening to turn the placemat. Trim the corners. Turn to the right side and press. Stitch the opening closed.

2. Topstitch 1/4" away from the finished edge, or quilt the placemat. We free-motion quilted ours, following the pattern in the fabric for the daisies and stripes.

Napkins
finished size 17 1/2" square

Cutting and Sewing instructions:

A standard napkin size is 18" square or 20" square. In our napkins we used the left over stripe fabric (the dahlia and fern portions) and pieced three sections together. If you are using one piece of fabric, cut the square and hem it on all four sides.

Because we chose to piece our napkins, we used a French seam to hide the raw edges. To make a French seam, place wrong sides of the fabric together and stitch a scant 1/4" seam. Fold the fabric right sides together and press the folded seam. Stitch again 1/4" from the folded edge.

Hem the outer edges by turning under a scant 1/4" and another 1/4" and topstitch in place.

Credits

Quilts designed by Valori & Jean Wells

Quilts sewn by Jean Wells, Valori Wells,
Pat Welsh, and Barbara Ferguson

Quilting by Barbara Ferguson and Shireen Hattan

Photography by Valori Wells

Book production and graphics by Lawry Thorn and Paige Vitek

The complete collection of Maraposa fabrics is shown on the opposite page.
All fabrics are also shown on our website:
http://www.stitchinpost.com/maraposa.asp

© Copyright June 2002 Jean Wells Keenan
Published by The Stitchin' Post

P.O. Box 280 • 311 W. Cascade • Sisters, OR 97759 • (541) 549-6061 • Fax (541) 549-1922 • www.stitchinpost.com

All rights reserved. No part of this book may be photocopied or reproduced without the express consent of The Stitchin' Post. All finished items produced from this book are protected by Federal Copyright Laws and may not be reproduced for commercial use in any form whatsoever without the express written consent of The Stitchin' Post.